Computer Networking

Fundamentals for Absolute Beginners

Alexander Bell

contained within this document, including, but not limited to, errors, omissions, or inaccuracies.

Table of Contents

Introduction

The year is 2019, and this side of the world is all consumed with whether Millennials are the better generation or not. Truth be told, there is no straight answer to that, but, fortunately, when it comes to the question "what is a computer network?", we have many answers. In fact, we can understand the concept and need for computer networks without any technical mumbo jumbo.

In ancient times, humans used to live in small, tight groups, like a pack of wolves. The survival rate was meager, and they had to move in search of food and shelter regularly. With time, humans realized that if they settle down in more significant numbers, it will benefit them in various ways. By building a society, they would be more protected from wild animal attacks and their harsh environments. Trade and commerce would become faster because instead of doing everything yourself or traveling long distances, most amenities were available at a stone's throw. This led to settlements that became villages, those became towns, the towns joined to form cities that later turned into states and eventually countries. On the highest level, these countries come together to create the world we live in today.

Computer networks were created for similar reasons: to join several computers together to accumulate their processing power. It helped in performing operations and providing services that were not possible otherwise. There are local networks, wide networks, wireless networks, layers upon layers of networks joining computers, and other devices. In this book, we are going to learn about the various layers that make up a typical computer network, and the devices, concepts, and protocols involved in creating such networks.

When I graduated with a computer engineering degree, computer networks was one of the major courses in my first semester. I am a person who finds abstract concepts hard to grasp. It is this reason why computer networks was such a hard course for me. You cannot see the working of a computer network visually and the mathematics involved is also quite confusing. But, thanks to the immense help from the course professor, I was able to ace the course and make a career as a computer engineer. In this book, I will try to keep things as simple as possible because it is essential to understand a concept before jumping to the next one. Everything is connected, after all, we are talking networks!

Chapter 1: Computer Networks & The Advent of the Internet

If you own a computer or cell phone, you must already have used a computer network. We are living in the digital age, and the internet is becoming a necessity more than a luxury as it was a decade ago. As with everything in this world, there are pros and cons to having a digital world. For example, you can now shop, maintain your bank accounts, talk with your friends and family, watch movies, get medical attention without leaving the comfort of your bed or couch. My cousin used to work in a telecommunications company as an RF engineer, and his job responsibilities were simple: find and fix network issues in the area allocated to him. As new technologies became available, the network evolved and gained capabilities to take care of optimization automatically. Result? My cousin and most RF engineers lost their jobs. Did they remain jobless forever? No, because they upgraded their skillset and got employed to maintain the new technologies.

Whenever a new technology becomes public, there is an adaptation curve. It takes time for people to learn and buy new technology. It takes even more time for engineers to optimize the new technology to make it less costly and have a better design. For example, remember how bulky, ugly, and expensive cell phones used to be? Compare that to the latest smartphones that you get for free with your cellular contracts.

Computer Networks

When you connect two or more computers, you get a network. You can either join the computers through a physical medium such as cables or a wireless medium, such as radio waves. Wireless networks are usually slower and have a smaller range. Keep in mind that computers are not just your laptop or your desktop. A mobile phone, or even your smartwatch is a computer. The different computer types used to create a network, the purpose of creating a network, and the medium used to join the computers, all these factors dictate the type of a network.

We are going to learn about different computer networks in detail in later chapters. For now, let's look at a few basic definitions.

Fundamentals

Protocols

Arguably the most commonly used word in the computer networks field, therefore it is very important to understand what protocols are. We have protocols in real-life too. Let me share a real-life experience that was embarrassing but taught me a very important lesson. In my first internship ever, every morning, the first thing I had to do was to generate a network report and email it. This is what the boss of my boss told me who was also the General Manager (GM) of the entire Southern network. It was my first day, and I forgot to ask who I should send it to. I couldn't ask anyone in my team because I was a little embarrassed, I started emailing the report to him directly every day! A whole week passed, and one day my team leader approached me and said I had to send it to a specific ID so my entire team would receive the report. My team lead said, "Even I don't directly email the GM!". This whole time the GM was forwarding emails to the team on my behalf, and I was just an intern! I was so embarrassed but also realized how nicely the GM handled the situation. He wanted to teach me about the chain of command and gave me a practical example by sending my immediate superior to relay the information instead of directly blasting me. That would have been catastrophic for an intern in his first week at a global corporation! What did I learn? In every workplace, there's a protocol (usually called the chain of command), which means you must report to your immediate superior and never bypass their authority. Only in special circumstances (such as to report any misconduct) would you contact the higher-ups. This protocol is also very important in the military code of conduct.

Different protocols are used to define various aspects of a particular network. There are several advantages, including:

1. Setting expectations: A protocol will determine how different network components will behave. It helps every element know beforehand what to expect from other components in every possible situation.
2. Communication rules: Protocol will also define which network component can communicate with which other components. This is very important to manage the network's security and resources.

We can say that to learn about a computer network is essentially learning about the many different protocols that define and govern that computer network.

Packet

A packet? Are we talking about a packet of candies? A packet of bacon-flavored chips? Unfortunately, (yet fortunately for your health), no. In a computer network, information is not sent altogether because it might be more than the network can transfer. For example, when you download a high-quality movie, it doesn't download in one go. Even with ultrafast fiber optic internet, it might take at least several seconds for the download to complete. In the background, what happens is that the information is broken down into small chunks and sent from the source to the destination. These small chunks of information are called packets.

The transmission rate (R) of a network is defined by the number of bits transferred per second from source to destination or the other way. If the packet to be sent has (L) number of bits, the time (T) required to completely transmit the packet will be T = L/R seconds.

The source adds a header to every packet it sends that contains information required to process that packet. When the packet is received at the destination, the header is always processed first to identify the packet properly.

Switching

A network is generally used to transmit different kinds of information. Sometimes, the source and/or destination change(s) in a network. How do we handle this multipurpose aspect of a network? We use switching. There are two main types of switching:

1. Packet switching
2. Circuit switching

In circuit switching, we have a dedicated/reserved network line (called a circuit) to complete every transmission. For the next transmission, a different circuit is created and used. A typical example of circuit switching would be the traditional landline phone every household used to have back in the day. When you made a call using the landline, the network created a link between you and the call receiver and maintained it during the entire call duration. Loss of that line connection resulted in a call drop. The constant connection resulted in a guaranteed transfer rate. Circuit switching is mostly used in analog networks.

In packet switching, the same network connection is used to handle all the communication. The network switches the transmission of different packets at a specific rate. An internet connection is the best example of packet switching. When you use the internet on your computer or smartphone, the connection rate is fixed and divided among the things you do over the internet. If you start a file download and stream a movie, it will seem both tasks are happening together. But in reality, your network switches transmission of packets from both tasks very quickly over the same connection. If you start doing a lot of things over the internet, you will experience a delay in completing some or all of the tasks. Packet switching is mostly prevalent in digital networks.

Modern-day networks combine packet and circuit switching to achieve the most optimum performance possible.

Delay

As mentioned earlier, a network can experience delays. Have you experienced stream buffering? Or a download that's stuck at the same percentage? That can happen due to a delay in the network. There can be different reasons why delays occur. Some of them are:

1. The system is busy in transmitting something else
2. A network component is either slow or not performing at all
3. Network capacity is reached

As you might have guessed already, depending upon why the delay happened, we can categorize delay into different types. Here are some very common delays present in almost all networks.

Processing Delay

The destination processes the packet header, so it knows what to do with the information in the packet. This creates a small delay because while the header is being processed, the information in the packet can't be used. If there are errors in the packet, the processing takes even more time as the errors are detected and fixed.

Queuing Delay

This delay is related to packet switching. This delay happens at the transmission source, where packets are waiting to be put in the transmission queue. Let's look at a real-life example: you are coming back from Walmart with groceries and want to make a right turn onto a road congested with traffic. You will have to wait until the traffic is cleared before you can make the turn. This is the queuing delay. We will discuss it in greater detail later in this book.

Transmission Delay

Another very common delay in all networks, the time it takes for the transmitter to send the packet, is called transmission delay. We have already established a formula to calculate that time, $T = L/R$. In most packet-switched networks, the transmission is performed on a first-come-first-served basis.

Depending upon the transmitter, the transmission delay can be between microseconds and milliseconds.

Propagation Delay

The time it takes for a packet to go from the source to the destination is called propagation delay. The further the source and destination, the greater this delay. It also depends upon the transmission medium, some transmission media, such as fiber optics, inherently support faster propagation than the others, such as coaxial cables. We can say the propagation delay is equal to the distance (d) between source and destination divided by the propagation speed (s) of the transmission medium ($T = d/s$).

Newcomers to computer networks always find it difficult to distinguish between transmission and propagation delay. Let's consider a real-life example to understand propagation and transmission delays. You and your friends are driving in three cars from Chicago to Toronto for a concert. The vehicles travel at a speed of 100 km/hr on the highway so it takes you around four hours to reach the Detroit border. The four hours is the propagation delay. The Canadian border patrol processes two cars every minute. There are already 25 cars waiting when your caravan of three vehicles reaches the border, bringing the total to 28 for processing. It took $28/2 = 14$ minutes for all vehicles carrying you and your friends to pass the border. This 14 minutes' delay is the transmission delay of the border crossing. It takes another four hours to reach Toronto. So, the total propagation delay from the source (Chicago) to destination (Toronto) was eight hours, and the transmission delay was 14 minutes.

It may take more time to transmit the packets than it takes them to propagate from transmitter to receiver. For example, a packet takes 5 seconds to propagate from source to destination, but the transmitter needs 10 seconds to transmit a packet. It means the first packet will reach the destination before the second packet is transmitted.

Nodal Delay

To understand nodal delay, we must first understand what a node is. A router, the source, the destination are all nodes in a network. The nodal delay (d_{nodal}) can be calculated by the following formula:

$$d_{nodal} = d_{proc} + d_{queue} + d_{trans} + d_{prop}$$

where d_{proc} is processing delay, d_{queue} is queueing delay, d_{trans} is transmission delay, d_{prop} is called propagation delay. Different delays contribute to different degrees towards the nodal delay and the proportions change from network to network.

The d_{proc}, d_{trans} and d_{prop} are highly dependent on the hardware configuration of the network. But, there is one delay, the d_{queue} which has been the focus of thousands of research studies and papers. The reason? Researchers want to find the most optimum way to queue packets that will result in minimum queuing delay and enhanced network performance. As you might have guessed, all these studies involve mathematical and statistical analysis as average, probability and variance are used to determine queueing delay and performance of a network.

Traffic Intensity

Traffic intensity is a measure of the rate at which packets join the queue (a), along with transmission rate (R) and the nature (size) of the packets (L). Mathematically, traffic intensity is given as $= La/R$.

Traffic intensity gives an idea about the queueing delay present in a network. If La/R > 1, it means the packets are arriving at the queue faster than they could be transmitted, the queue will keep growing and queuing delay will keep creeping towards infinity. Of course, all working networks keep the traffic intensity less than 1.

If La/R ≤ 1, there will be no queuing delay if each packet arrives after L/R seconds. If packets are arriving in after L/R but in bursts, first burst will not experience any queuing delay, but the second will experience L/R delay, third burst will have 2L/R, and so on. We can generalize delay for the nth burst as $(n - 1)$ L/R.

In reality, the packets randomly arrive at the queue. The time interval between packets is random. But, the La/R is sufficient enough to understand the concept of traffic intensity in a computer network.

Loss

When the source transmits complete information, but the receiver receives partial information, it's termed as a (transmission/packet) loss. Every network experiences a range of losses, mostly due to the limitations of physical components involved in a network. There are various error checking and correction protocols that networks implement to detect and fix losses so the receiver gets the complete information sent by the source. But, there are times when the loss is so bad there's no way to fix the issue. How many times have you made a video call only to see a very pixelated video or listen to a robotic voice? These things usually happen due to a bad connection that results in a lot of packet loss.

Error

Sometimes the receiver receives all the packets, but the information is not what the source sent. This is because an external element affected the packets during the sending, transmission, or reception stage and changed the information it was carrying. You can argue that loss is a form of error, which is technically correct, but usually, when we say error, we refer to situations when incorrect information is received at the destination. All modern computer networks have error detection and correction mechanism in place. But, as with all man-made systems, there is always a possibility of errors happening. One of the biggest examples is online multiplayer games. You might have seen players complaining while playing first-person shooter games that they shot someone squarely in the head, only for it to register partial damage. In such high data transfer scenarios, even a 0.1% error rate can result in a very bad user experience (UX).

Throughput

The throughput is one of the most common parameters used to determine the performance of a computer network. Whenever you download a file over the internet, you see the download speed, which is usually given as x kB/s or MB/s, which means your computer is receiving the file at a rate of x kilobytes/megabytes per second. This rate is called the network throughout. Depending upon specific application needs, the system might compromise on delay or throughput to provide the best experience. For example, in a video call, it's better to have a low-quality video with minimum delay rather than a high-quality video with a major delay.

Knowing all the fundamental definitions makes it easier to understand how computer networks evolved over the decades to become what they are today, and that's exactly what we will cover now.

Bits, Bytes and Data Rate Units

A digital system is a binary system that means there are only two possible states, on or off. These states are denoted by the numbers 1 and 0, called bits. To denote real-world information in a digital system, a combination of 8 bits called byte was formulated. As computers started to handle more and more data, it was time to come up with bigger units. A kiloByte (kB) is 1024 bytes, which is 8192 bits. A MegaByte (MB) is similarly 1024 kiloBytes. Currently, computer systems can handle GigaBytes (GB) of data, and each GB is 1024 MBs itself. There are storage devices that can contain TeraBytes (TB) of data, and each TB is 1024 GBs.

When we talk about data in computer networks, we are usually referring to the number of bits (or bytes) transferred, processed or received by a single node over time (often in seconds). Modern networks can also handle big data rates, for example, a typical fast ethernet connection today can support up to 10 Gbps.

History of Computer Networks

Computer networks have evolved considerably over the years. Initially created for high-level applications, the bulk now happens in the public domain. Let's take a look at the history.

1961: Leonard Kleinrock proposes one of the earliest ideas of a computer network, ARPANET, in his paper "Information Flow in Large Communication Nets."

1962: Telstar, an active communications satellite, is launched and successfully receives and transmits inter-continental communications. By active satellite, I mean a satellite that amplifies the received signal before forwarding to the destination.

1965: Donald Davies coins the term "packet" for data sent between computers in a network.

1969: This is an eventful year for computer networks.

1- ARPANET officially comes to life when the University of California, Los Angeles (UCLA) and Stanford Research Institute (SRI) are connected as the first two nodes of the network. On August 29, 1969, the first-ever Interface Message Processor (IMP) and network switch were received by UCLA. The setup is later used to transmit the very first data collection over the ARPANET.

2- The first of its kind, a document called Request for Comments (RFC) that defined and discussed the intricacies of computer networks and the involved procedures and protocols, is released.

1970: Steve Crocker releases the file-sharing protocol NetWare Core Protocol (NCP), working with a UCLA team.

1971: Ray Tomlinson sends the first email. The Hawaiian Islands are connected through a wireless Ultra High Frequency (UHF) packet network called ALOHAnet. This network will later help lay the foundation of WiFi.

1973: Another year with a lot of progress in the field of computer networks.

1- Robert Metcalfe, a Xerox PARC employee, develops Ethernet.

2- ARPA deploys the first international network connection called SATNET linking with University College London (UCL).

3- The VoIP technology with initial capabilities is devised, and an experimental VoIP call is made, which results in success. It is interesting to note that until 1995 the technology remained unavailable to the public domain.

1974: Routers are used for the first time by Xerox. These routers, however, vary greatly from the present day routers and not considered IP routers.

1976: Gateway is developed by Ginny Strazisar, which is the first true IP router.

1978: Bob Kan invents the TCP/IP protocol, and with the help of Vint Cerf, successfully develops it for networks.

1981: Another big year for computer networks as significant strides are made in network design and protocols.

1- RFC 791 officially defines Internet Protocol version 4 (IPv4), which is the first significant collection of internet protocols. It is still in use.

2- BITNET is created as a network to connect IBM mainframe systems across the United States.

3- US National Science Foundation develops the Computer Science Network (CSNET).

1983: ARPANET is converted to use TCP/IP. Paul Mockapetris and Jon Postel implement the first DNS.

1986: National Science Foundation Network (NSFNET) comes online. It was originally the ARPANET's backbone, but in the early 1990s replaced it. The bandwidth issues with BITNET are resolved with the introduction of BITNET II.

1988: A lot of things happened this year.

1- T1 backbone is added to ARPANET for the first time.

2- AT&T, Lucent, and NCR introduce WaveLAN technology, which proved to be the precursor to WiFi networks.

3- A paper is released that discusses the first-ever firewall technology. Created by Digital Equipment Corporation (DEC), it is called a packet filter firewall.

4- The first Transatlantic fiber-optic cable TAT-8 is laid down by a joint venture of AT&T Corporation, France Télécom, and British Telecom.

1990: A US network hardware company, Kalpana, introduces the first-ever network switch.

1996: IPv6 is released to improve various aspects of IPv4, including embedded encryption, improved routing, and a wider range of IP addresses.

1997: The first version of WiFi 802.11 standard is introduced in June. It supports up to 2 Mbps of transmission speeds.

1999: Another big year for computer networks.

1- The 802.11a WiFi standard is officially released that uses a 5 GHz frequency band that supports speeds up to 25 Mbps.

2- During mid-1999, the public gets access to devices compatible with the 802.11b standard supporting transmission speeds up to 11 Mbps.

3- In September 1999, Wired Equivalent Privacy (WEP) protocol is introduced to enable encryption on WiFi networks.

2003: After a couple of years of not much progress, a lot of new things happen this year.

1- 802.011g standard is released in public-domain supporting transmission speeds of up to 20 Mbps.

2- A new encryption protocol is introduced for 802.11g called the WiFi Protected Access WPA.

3- Enhanced encryption on WiFi networks is made possible with the introduction of an improved WPA2 protocol. The deadline was set in 2006 for all devices using WiFi technology to comply with the new encryption protocol.

2009: 802.11n WiFi standard is officially released. It supports faster transmission speeds on a dual-bandwidth system of 2.4 GHz and 5 GHz frequency bands. This is the WiFi standard currently in use all over the world.

2018: WPA3 encryption protocol is introduced for even better security on WiFi networks.

Communication is an important factor in armed conflicts. If you read the history of wars and battles fought in the last century, you will know how vital consistent and secured communication really is in determining the outcome. Most network technologies currently in the public domain are considered obsolete for military applications. The technologies used by militaries are usually 10-15 generations more advanced than what is available to the public.

What Is the Internet?

Have you thought about how vast the internet is? Millions, possibly billions of devices (or components), connected together to provide a single service. It is also arguably the largest system completely engineered by mankind. Even though it's such a huge and complex system, it's not that difficult to understand how it works. I think that is because the internet is a tiered or layered system. Each layer can be studied independently one at a time, so it does not get overwhelming for people who are learning about computer networks for the first time. We can describe the internet in two different ways.

From a Hardware Perspective

As I already mentioned, the internet is a network that combines millions of hardware components around the world. In today's world, everything from your smartphone to your printer to your security system is connected to the internet. We can say that the internet has evolved and not just a 'computer' network. Each component is either called a host or end system. In Oct 2019, around 4.48 billion people had active access to the internet (Clement, 2019). We know that there are different components like switches and routers that help in maintaining a connection over the internet. Let's consider the internet as a link between two computers with a router between them. The sublink A has computer A as the host and the router as an end system, while sublink B has a router as host and computer B as the end system.

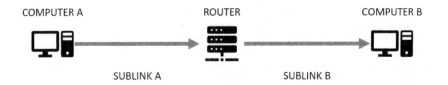

COMPUTER A   ROUTER   COMPUTER B

SUBLINK A   SUBLINK B

Since there are millions of devices that need to connect, all of them must follow the same protocols to avoid any conflict. This is made sure by ensuring compliance of the devices to a certain standard. These standards, also known as RFCs, are now formulated by the Internet Engineering Task Force (IETF).

From a Service Perspective

It will not be wrong to say that the internet is a giant infrastructure created to provide services to applications. Applications that users can use to do things they want to do. For example, the internet is essential for all web applications, including but not limited to emails, web browsing, video streaming, to work correctly. The applications are run on end systems of the internet and are referred to as distributed applications. If you want to develop a distributed system, you can focus on the application requirement and user experience without thinking much about the network constraints. You don't have to worry about the routers and switches or the transmission link that will be used, you just create the application and the end systems can utilize it. The worldwide web (www) applications have three main design components, two static and one dynamic.

1. HTML
2. CSS
3. JavaScript

Every application also supports an Application Programming Interface (API) that enables other applications and end systems to communicate with the application. We will discuss Internet API later in greater detail. If you want to understand this concept using a real-world analogy, we can consider the postal service. When you write a letter to someone else, you just don't write it and throw it out your window or put it in a glass bottle and let the ocean waves take it. I mean, you can certainly do these things depending on the situation, but if you want the letter to reach its destination, you will have to follow the instructions set by your local post office. You have to put the letter in an envelope, seal it, put a stamp in the top right-hand corner and address it accordingly. You must then drop it at the post office or in a designated mailbox. The postal service doesn't only courier letters for you; they also handle packages and cargo. All this is pretty similar when we talk about the Internet.

Network Architecture

Every computer network has a set architecture that is usually designed to fulfill the needs of the specific application. In general, there are two major types of network architectures.

Peer to Peer (P2P) Architecture

A network where all the computers share the burden of completing a task. There is no overall hierarchy in the network, although different computers might assume different responsibilities at a given time. There is no central server to provide instructions and resources.

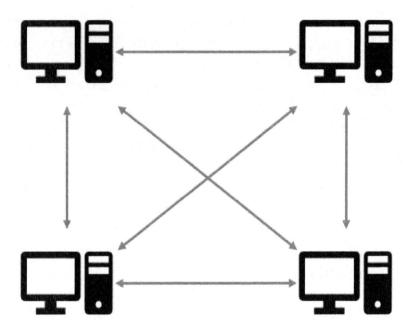

A very good example of a P2P network is the torrent network. Although it is used mostly to distribute pirated digital content these days, it is a very efficient and cheap system to distribute resources. The required files reside on computers where the user has accepted to *seed* the files. In most situations, multiple seeders are present. The users who want to download (*leech*) the file connect directly to the seeders' computers and perform the download. The whole operation is facilitated by a P2P client (software/application). We are going to take a closer look at how P2P networks work later in this book.

Advantages

- Less costly due to the absence of a dedicated server
- Lack of a central command means there's a lot of redundancy meaning the network will keep working even if one peer fails

- Modern computers have simplified protocols that make P2P community grow significantly

Disadvantages

- Lack of a controlling server poses security risks
- Data backups and consistency check-ups need to be done on every peer
- Performance degrades as the number of peers grows in a network especially if they are physically far apart

Client/Server Architecture

A highly powerful computer acts as the server controlling all the aspects of a system. Other computers can connect to the network if allowed by the server and take advantage of the services provided. These computers are called clients.

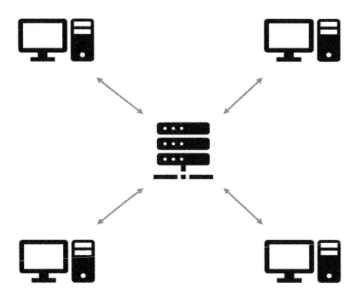

Clients cannot communicate with each other directly unless allowed by the server. Most online services you use have this architecture. We can use online multiplayer games as another good example, where you connect to a gaming server and play with other players. All the clients interact with each other in real-time, but everything passes through the server. Some clients (players) use cheats to bypass server control and do things they are not supposed to. It is the responsibility of the game developers to regularly update their servers so such activities are stopped and bad clients banned from using the server again.

Advantages

- Better security and control over the network
- Servers handle the brunt of operation load that means clients can use simpler devices to enjoy high-quality services as long as they have a good connection with the server

Disadvantages

- Servers are expensive because they have to handle the entire load of the network
- The entire network is affected if the server goes down. For this reason, most services have redundant servers that increase the cost even more
- More technical staff is required to maintain the server

You might be wondering if it is so expensive to manage servers, how is it that more and more companies are focusing on online services? This is enabled by third-party server services that provide affordable and scalable server services to companies that do not want to create and maintain their own servers. For example, a mobile gaming company will get services from

Amazon Web Services (AWS) for a fixed monthly cost. The company will not have to create their own servers and also will not need to hire extra manpower for server maintenance.

We can discuss the architecture in terms of the layers present in the network design. The most commonly known network layer model is the Open Systems Interconnection (OSI) model, which is the focus of study in this book. As we have already discussed, computer networks are very complex systems, and to make it easier to understand; it is split into theoretical layers.

If you think about it, most systems you interact with in life can be divided into layers according to some criteria. For example, how would you explain if your friend asks you how did you get your driving license (I hope he's not asking it after seeing you drive!)? You can explain the complex process by dividing the actions into groups. Here are the groups:

1. Give written test
2. Take driving classes
3. Book driving test
4. Give driving test
5. Get a driver's license

| TEST | LESSONS | SCHEDULE | TEST | LICENSE |

We know that the above five steps are a simplified version of a number of sub-actions you took to get your license. For example, let's look at an expanded version of each action group:

1. Give written test
   a. Book your test by paying the fee
   b. Prepare for the test
   c. Go to the testing center on the test date
   d. Give the test and hopefully pass it
   e. Get the temporary license and wait for the actual card in the mail
2. Take driving classes
   a. Find a good driving instructor possibly someone who can issue you a certificate
   b. Take paid lessons until you feel confident or the instructor gives you the green light
3. Book driving test
   a. Book the driving test online or by visiting the driving test center. Book a time in the morning, so there is a minimum wait time, and you can take time off from work
   b. Clear your schedule on the test date. If you work, ask your boss for permission to come a few hours late
4. Give driving test
   a. Reach the test center around 15-30 minutes early
   b. Give the driving test and ace it
   c. Get the temporary license and wait for the actual card in the mail

Truth be told, we still haven't mentioned a lot of small things that you must do in each activity group. But, you get the gist. This is the same concept when we use layers to define a network architecture.

OSI Model

There is one more advantage of dividing a network into theoretical layers. It helps in standardizing a network irrespective of the internal details. It helps the integration of different networks that have the same structure model. This is the same concept when you build products for the general masses. For example, a chair is a piece of furniture that can be used by anyone who can sit. No matter if the chair is made of metal, wood, or plastic, if the person is old or of a different race, the chair is compatible with all humans. But even with this standardization or generalization, there are some requirements needed for both systems to work together.

The OSI model has seven layers.

1. Application layer
2. Presentation Layer
3. Session Layer
4. Transport Layer
5. Network Layer
6. (Data) Link Layer
7. Physical Layer

Chapter 2: Application Layer

The application layer is the one that users interact with. We can also say that the application layer forms the interface of a computer network. It is also not wrong to say networks are created to serve the applications that run on this layer.

Before we move forward, let us clear one confusion. In OSI model, the applications in whole are not considered part of the application layer. The part of the application that provides an interface between the application and the next layer of the network (which is "Presentation" in OSI model), and with other applications is considered application layer. This is the case for all layers in the OSI model; the responsibilities and capabilities of each layer are very narrowed down (or specific/precise).

Fundamentals

Let's pause for a moment and think about how far we have progressed when it comes to the online applications in use today. The access is easy, cheap, and have lesser requirements. I still remember the first time I bought a computer and connected it to the internet. It was a top-of-the-line dialup connection with the worst static noise you could ever hear. It was insanely expensive with crazy download and upload limits. I could only download and upload 100 MBs of data with a maximum speed of 25 kbps. What did I used it for? I sent and received emails. I read the news on a website. Today, I have a gigabit fiber-to-home connection with unlimited download and upload quota. I just checked before and downloaded around 600 GBs of data. I had no idea I was such a heavy internet user. But, it makes sense when you think about it. One HD movie is approximately 2 GBs of data stream. There are software updates on your computer, and, if you are a gamer like me, you know that just a small game update these days is in the range of 25-40 GBs of data download.

"Necessity is the mother of invention" is very true when it comes to the relation between applications and how user demand pushed engineers and scientists to come up with better network technologies. But, there's a hint of reverse logic here as well. Better technology enabled people to create better applications. Instead of Tetris, you create Unravel, instead of Orkut, you create Facebook, instead of MSN/Yahoo Messenger, you create Skype. Not that there's anything wrong with those classics, it's just that you can do more when you know there is an infrastructure to support it.

In simple terms, the purpose of the application layer is to convert data from a format that's useful to the end-user to a format that's ready for the network. Every application you use for performing online tasks has all the necessary capabilities built-in to work as an application layer. What are those capabilities? We are going to discuss some now.

HTTP

The HyperText Transfer Protocol (HTTP) is the basis of every website and web application you visit and use online. Internet (or the World Wide Web) is a giant network interconnecting millions of client/server networks. It started as a private network between academics linking students, professors across universities, and launched to the public domain in the early 90s. It has since then become the umbrella network enabling all other networks to rely on its resources to perform their tasks. HTTP allows you to use an application and request information that is stored somewhere else. Depending upon the privileges server has given you, you can view or edit the information.

HTTP is an unsecured protocol that is a big security concern, especially if it's used to interact with resources that have sensitive information such as e-commerce sites. To enhance security and add encryption, a secure HTTPS version was released that is now the standard for all websites.

Before we dive into the working of HTTP, we need to understand a few things.

IP Address

Everything connected to the internet has a unique identification number, called the Internet Protocol (IP) address. When you get internet from an Internet Service Provider (ISP), you are assigned an IP address that acts as your address on the internet, similar to your mailing address. It is unique to you, and people can physically locate you using your IP address. Some services mask your IP address online if you wish to, and your ISP is responsible for keeping your IP address private.

Want to check your IP address? If you are on a Windows 10 computer, click on 'Start', search 'cmd' and open 'Command Prompt'. Run the command 'ipconfig'. You will see a bunch of information that will include IPv6 and IPv4 addresses. You might be wondering why there are both addresses, and it is because many online services still use that protocol. One of the reasons IPv6 was introduced was because IPv4 used 8 numbers (32 bits) which limits the number of possible IP addresses to exactly 4,294,967,296 (roughly more than 4 billion), it's a big number but still not enough for all the devices connected to the internet. On the other hand, IPv6 creates addresses from 128 bits that makes the available IP addresses to be 340 undecillion.

You don't know how many zeros are in an undecillionth? That's 340,000,000,000,000,000,000,000,000,000,000,000,000 possible IP addresses!

Website

A website is a resource stored on a remote server that you can access using a client-side application if that server allows it. For example, to visit the website of Google, you need an internet browser on your computer. You also need to know the address of Google's website, and of course an active internet connection.

We have to remember that in every client/server network, the client-side application has to provide an interface to the user and process data from human-readable form to machine-readable form and vice versa. Depending upon the information received from the server, the client might also perform some processing that doesn't concern the server. For example, the website you requested would like to show you your current time. Instead of the server requesting your computer your current time and then relaying that information back to your browser, the server will instruct your browser to get the current time from your computer and show it on your screen.

It is also interesting to note that, in most cases, the server doesn't keep a record of the HTTP requests made by a client. Therefore, HTTP is a *stateless* protocol. The server will respond to every HTTP request sent by a client, even if it's redundant.

This opens the possibility of malicious attacks because a client might make so many requests; the server will get overwhelmed and unresponsive. To avoid that, most servers today limit the number of requests a client can make at a specific time.

The root folder on the server is what you access when you enter the domain name of a website. A website is a collection of web pages that are files on the root folder. You might also have subfolders in the directory that you can also access by adding the path to the domain name.

URL

Remember, when we said everything connected to the internet has an IP address? How bad would it be if you had to enter the IP address of the server that contains the website to view it? To make things simpler for the end-user, the server IP addresses have been replaced by Universal Resource Locator (URL). We enter the URL in the browser, and it takes care of finding, connecting, and transferring information from that server. There are different components of a URL. We are going to discuss the two most important ones.

Protocol and 'www'

The protocol that should be used to connect to the website, which is, of course, HTTP or HTTPS in case of secure websites. In modern browsers, you do not need to enter the protocol or the 'www' of the URL; the browser will attempt to resolve it automatically.

Domain Name

This is the unique name that is assigned to every website along with a type ('.com,' '.net,' etc.). It is like creating a nickname for your physical address. There are domain sellers from whom you have to buy a domain. The domain seller will allocate the domain name to you if it's available, maintain the domain name records and link it with the server IP address.

There are other components, but we will leave them for now. You can also host your server and maintain your domain name records. This is how things used to be back in the day, but nowadays, most people find it easier to get these services from a provider.

Path

As mentioned before, the files on the server can be stored either in the root folder or in a subfolder. You can access a file present in a subfolder by appending its path to the domain name.

DNS

When you enter a URL in the browser, the browser looks up the domain name in a set of files containing domain records maintained by your ISP in a Domain Name Server (DNS) to resolve it and find the server's IP address. The set of files is called zone files. If no server address is found for the domain name, you will get an error on your browser.

When you update your DNS records, or if you change the server's IP address that the domain name must resolve to, it takes time, usually 48-72 hours, for the changes to make it to various ISP records. Until then, the domain name might not resolve correctly. When you visit a website for the first time, the domain records are resolved and cached, so for future requests, there will be no need to find what the server's IP address is.

Socket and Port

HTTP uses TCP/IP to transport data in the network. We know that at a given time, different applications and services are running on a computer that is using the internet. To make things easier to separate the data, different ports are assigned to different application data. For example, port 80 is usually reserved for all internet traffic. Imagine you are living in an apartment building, your building has a fixed street address shared by all apartments, but, for the postal service to correctly deliver stuff to everyone, they need to exact apartment number as well. This is the same concept used in IP address and port numbers. The combination of an IP address and a specific port is called a socket.

Port numbers are created using a 16-bit number; therefore, the port number can between the range of 0 to 65535 decimal numbers. Some port numbers are reserved for special purposes. The rest are available to be used for custom applications.

The Working of HTTP

Let's see how HTTP actually works. You might already have a rough idea after all the topics discussed above. There is one more concept involved in HTTP protocol, the persistency of the connection. Depending upon the application requirements, a persistent connection must be maintained between the client and server. For example, a streaming application will need a persistent connection between the server and the client for the streaming to keep working. Other applications do not require a consistent connection work.

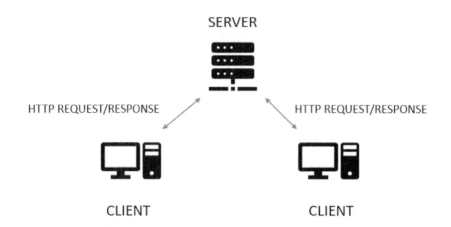

SERVER

HTTP REQUEST/RESPONSE   HTTP REQUEST/RESPONSE

CLIENT   CLIENT

Non-persistent connection

Let's take an example of you opening the Google search engine website, https://www.google.com/. Here's what will happen on the background.

1- Browser will initiate a TCP connection to Google's server using port 80

2- After a successful connection, the browser will send an HTTP request to the server containing information about the requested request

3- The server processes the HTTP request, fetches the required resources, wraps it in an HTTP response, and sends it to the client. Also requests the connection be closed but the connection remains open until client-side acknowledges reception of the resource

4- The client receives the HTTP response, and the client-server connection is terminated.

5- The resource (which is an HTML file) might have references for other resources such as images and videos. The client replays the steps 1-4 for each of those resources.

The browser might process and show resources in different ways. That has nothing to do with the HTTP. Note that the resources are shown to the user as they are available, heavier files take longer to transfer from server to client, it is this reason that sometimes you might see the web page and text while the images and videos are still loading. It means that the requests are asynchronous, the request does not block one another, and in modern websites, many HTTP requests are processed simultaneously for faster website load speed.

Persistent connection

The biggest problem with a non-persistent connection is that the connection is created and ended for every resource. It's a waste of precious time and resources as both server and client have to maintain buffers to maintain consistency. This can be a huge burden on the server as it has to maintain a connection with millions of clients.

The above problems are solved by keeping a persistent connection between the server and client. But, the issue here is the capacity of the server. Imagine millions of viewers watching Netflix at the same time, and there is no way a single server can handle persistent connection for all the clients. The solution is to have a data center that will divide traffic among multiple servers. On top of that, there are redundant data centers to make sure if one data center fails, the service doesn't get interrupted.

HTTP Response Codes

If you have used the internet for some time, you must have seen some of the codes mentioned below.

1xx - Information Responses

Any HTTP response that starts with number '1' is an information response. You might not have seen these. These are used by client and server to pass information between them.

2xx - Successful Responses

Used to transmit when requests have been successfully processed. The most common is the Code 200 'OK,' which means the HTTP request was completed.

3xx - Redirection Responses

When the resource has moved to a new location on the server, these responses are used. The most common is the Code 301 'Permanent Redirect' which tells the resource is moved and also gives the new location of the resource.

4xx - Client Error Responses

These are produced when an error happens on the client-side. The most common is Code 404 'Not Found,' which means the server wasn't able to find the resource requested by the client.

5xx - Server Error Responses

These error codes are seen if the server encountered an error. The most common is the Code 503 'Service Unavailable' which means the server could not handle the request. The most common cause is the server being down or overloaded. If you have done online shopping one a website during a crazy sale event, you might have seen the website shows this error a few times.

Caching and Cookies

There are a few techniques that can make a non-persistent connection faster. The techniques are caching and cookies.

Caching

Several resource types, especially media files such as images and videos, require the most time to get from server to client due to their large file sizes. These are also the most repeated content on a website; the same images usually appear on several pages on a website. The browser creates a cache using the available memory on the client and temporarily saves these resources. When the subsequent requests are made for the same resources, instead of requesting them from the server again, they are served from the cache. It greatly speeds up the process of serving a web page to the user.

Cookies

A server also sometimes needs to get a response from the client to know what needs to be done next. For example, the server might need to authenticate the user using a username and password to show private information. Instead of asking for the login credentials every time you access some private information, your login status can be saved in a cookie for a time, and the server will show you the information without asking for authentication. This not only speeds up the process, but it also helps the user avoid nuisance for the user to authenticate and waste time every time some private information is needed in a short time.

Cookies have expiry dates, and it means they are deleted automatically after a preset time. Caches, on the other hand, are kept until the user clears the cache. In modern client applications, the cache is smartly managed. You can set the amount of memory to be used as a cache and choose to delete entries that you haven't accessed in some time.

Before we move onto the next topic, let's talk about a problem that caching creates. You access a photography website, and your browser caches all the images in the cache. After some time, the images are changed on the server. But, you will keep seeing the older images because your browser will continue accessing them from the local cache instead of requesting them from the server. Usually, you have the option to run a command and force browser to request updated resources from the server, but how you would know the images have changed on the server? As a website developer, this is a serious problem. Luckily, there are several ways the server can force the browser to request a specific resource from it instead of using it from the local cache. One of them is version control, it's a bit out of the scope of this book, but you can research it online.

FTP

The File Transfer Protocol (FTP) is a protocol to transfer, drum rolls please, files. Yes, that was a duh moment. An FTP connection is usually created between a fixed client/server network. The goal is to access the files, possibly download and update them (if the server allows these operations). There are dedicated FTP client applications; one of the most popular is the Filezilla.

The user will use the FTP client application to make a connection to the remote server. It means the server will already have set up the user account on its side and the resources that account can access. The user will need the authentication information set by the server to make the connection. It will include server address and port number, username, and password. When the client initiates the link, this information is sent to the server for authentication. If it matches what server has on its side, the server accepts the connection request and opens it for the client to access the files.

FTP is similar to HTTP in the sense that both request and fetch files. But there are some differences.

1- In FTP, upon successful authentication, two connections are established between client and server. One is the control connection that is used to transmit requests, responses, and other system information about the connection. This connection always remains open until either client or server ends the connection (persistent). The other is the data connection, which is used to send files back and forth. This connection only opens when a file needs to be transferred (non-persistent). Both connections use different ports.

2- FTP connection is not stateless like HTTP, so the server has to maintain a record of the state of the client actively. Therefore, FTP requires considerable resources on the server-side, and servers usually have a limit to the FTP accounts that can simultaneously connect.

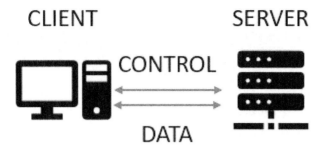

CLIENT   SERVER

CONTROL

DATA

SMTP

Electronic mails (emails) have been one of the basic tenets of the internet, even before the internet became mainstream. Emails are an essential form of communication over the internet and have become more versatile over time. Emails work just like sending letters through the postal service, i.e., it is not a real-time communication system. The sender and receiver use the system at their convenience, making emails an asynchronous communication channel. You can use any email service as long as you are connected to the internet and have signed up for a particular email service provider. The email service is always free, although there are paid services that offer more features (or do not show ads). You can add attachments to an email, which can be a file, or another email (which is called email forwarding).

One of the most popular email client applications is Microsoft Outlook, which is widely used by businesses. Let's take an example where Martin (martin@outlook.com) uses Microsoft Outlook to send an email to his business partner Tim who uses Google Mail (tim@gmail.com).

1- Martin sends an email that goes to the Outlook SMTP servers.

2- Outlook SMTP servers detect that it needs to go to the Gmail SMTP server. Outlook will request a TCP connection with Gmail, which will be granted after an initial handshaking process.

3- Once the connection is set up, Outlook will transfer Martin's email to the Gmail server.

4- Now, two things can happen depending upon the settings the receiver has set.

a- Tim has set email retrieving to FETCH - which means Gmail client will only get the emails from the server when the receiver starts the client or instructs the client to get the emails.

b- Tim has set email retrieving to PUSH - which means the email server will forward all emails addressed to the receiver to its client as soon as the server receives the email.

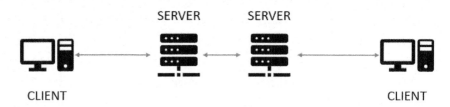

SMTP was developed well before HTTP, and it was in use as early as the 1980s. At that time, connections only allowed restricted content to be sent. Nowadays, you can do all kinds of things in an email, which has actually given rise to two types of emails you can compose. The classic *plain* email, which contains simple unformatted text and the modern *HTML* email, where you can use apply various formatting styles to the email body text. But, even with the HTML type, the subject can only contain plain text created with American Standard Code for Information Interchange (ASCII) characters.

P2P

We already talked about the architecture of P2p networks because they differ from the usual client/server networks. We will now look into the workings and some mathematics involved in P2P on the application layer.

Consider that we have to distribute a large-sized file (with a size of F bits) over a P2P network. Remember that in a P2P network, the server containing the file is a peer, much like the hosts/clients seeking the file. It means any client that has received a portion of the file can start redistributing to other clients that don't have that portion. In other words, as more clients have access to the file, the easier it gets for the remaining clients to get the file. We can also say that P2P is a self-scalable network. Let's say the upload rate of the first peer to have the file (for ease we are going to call it server) is u_s, the upload rate of the ith peer is u_i, and the download rate of ith peer is u_i. The total number of peers in the network seeking the file is denoted by N. The download rate of the peer with the slowest one is denoted by d_{min}. Let's consider that the other peers will not contribute towards uploading the file. In that case, the minimum distribution time D_s, will be more than, or equal to the larger of the two following parameters.

1- File must be transmitted at least once to each of the N peers, which means NF bits must be transmitted in total by the server. The minimum time to distribute the file will be NF/u_s because the upload speed of the server is u_s.

2- The peer with the slowest download rate will have the minimum distribution time, given as F/d_{min}.

Mathematically, we can write minimum distribution time as

$$Ds \geq \max\left\{\frac{NF}{u_s}, \frac{F}{d_{min}}\right\}$$

In a P2P connection, the minimum distribution parameters are a bit different.

1- The minimum distribution time is given by the time it needs for the server to send the file to one of the peers because from that point forward, the peers can redistribute the files themselves. The minimum time, therefore, becomes F/u_s.

2- The minimum distribution time for the peer with the slowest download rate remains the same F/d_{min}.

3- Remember that in P2p network, each peer becomes a server as soon as it receives a chunk of the file, the total upload time of the network as a whole gets increased by the upload time of each peer over time. We can denote this by $u_{total} = u_s + u_1 + ... + u_N$. In this case, the NF/u_{total}.

Mathematically, we can write minimum distribution time as

$$D_{P2P} \geq \max\left\{\frac{F}{u_s}, \frac{F}{d_{min}}, \frac{NF}{u_s + \sum_{i=1}^{N} u_i}\right\}$$

Chapter 3: Presentation Layer

The presentation layer, also known as the syntax layer, is officially the translator of the network. This layer makes the data presentable for the application layer through services like conversion and encoding, enhances networking security through encryption, and even improve network performance through compression. Let's look at all these services.

Services

Data Conversion

Data conversion is the process of changing the format of data. All digital systems work on binary numbers that make little to no sense to human end-users. The biggest task of the presentation layer is to convert the binary data transmitted through the network to a format that the application layer can use.

When dealing with data conversion, there are few rules related to information theory that should be remembered.

1- It is easier to discard data but very difficult to add missing data. For example, it's very easy to convert a colored image to grayscale but very difficult to do the reverse

2- There are different algorithms to replace missing data, but in most cases, human end-user must choose how to handle such situations. Research studies are going on in the field of artificial intelligence to make this process completely automatic

3- It is easier and faster to modify and analyze digital data

In any case, the better conversion practice is to use a middle-state when converting from one format to another instead of performing direct conversion between the two formats. It helps in homogenizing conversion of different formats leading to the use of the same conversion system for various conversions. This technique is called a pivotal conversion. For example, an audio converter may convert audio data from FLAC format to AAC by using PCM as a middle-state. It is important to remember that losses frequently happen during conversion.

Character Code Translation

There are different methods to encode data when converting from one format (or type) to another. There is a long list of character codes currently in use today, some of the most common are.

1- ASCII

2- Unicode (UTF-8, UTF-16, UTF-32)

3- MS Windows character set

4- ISO 8859-character set

In communication systems, the concept of line coding (sometimes also referred to as data mapping) is used to represent binary data with voltage or current (sometimes photons) patterns. Some of the common encoding methods include polar, unipolar, and bipolar codes. For example, consider the binary string 1101110. One way to encode this data would be to use +ve voltage/current value for 1 and -ve voltage/current value for 0. Another way is to switch voltage/current polarity only when the bit changes, different encoding helps in different applications. We also have to remember that transmitting voltage/current states over long distances can be different as various factors affect levels.

Compression

The purpose of compression is to use fewer bits to represent the original data before transmission, so it uses fewer resources and requires less distribution time. Compression is called source coding when applied to facilitate data transmission in a network. There are basically two types of compression.

1- Lossless compression reduces data bits through the identification and removal of redundancies. In most cases, not much compression can be achieved through lossless compression

2- Lossless compression reduces data by dropping some useful bits that might not be noticeable at the receiver's end. For example, audio might be compressed from 512 kbps to 32 kbps before transmission and the client might not even notice the difference. The same thing can be applied to videos with decompression techniques deployed on the client's end to reproduce the video in its original quality. Compression and decompression processes require time and resources, so there's always a tradeoff.

Encryption and Decryption

I still remember when I used to call my high school girlfriend using our home landline, and my mom would sometimes eavesdrop from the other phone set in the kitchen. The current generation is so lucky that's not the case anymore, at least with the communication possibilities they have now, such as cellular networks and the internet. Everything that is transmitted in modern networks is heavily encrypted and almost impossible to hack unless you have the proper authority to access it. However, there have been reports of data interception in networks that do not deploy the latest encryption protocols.

Sublayers

The presentation layer can be divided into two sublayers, Common Application Service Element (CASE) and Specific Application Service Element (SASE).

CASE

A lot of applications require the same services from the next layer in the OSI model, which is the session layer. This sublayer provides all such common services. One such service is the Association Control Service Element (ACSE) that enables different applications to communicate. It verifies the application identities and can also run authentication checks if needed.

SASE

As the name suggests, this sublayer fulfills services related to specific applications. Some of these services include File Transfer, Access and Manager (FTAM), Virtual Terminal (VT), and Remote Database Access (RDA).

Chapter 4: Session Layer

The fifth layer of the OSI model is the session layer. The purpose of this layer is to maintain a session between different end-user applications to facilitate the transmission of requests and responses.

Services

The session layer provides authentication, authorization, check pointing, and recovery services to applications communicating with each other.

Authentication and Authorization

One of the most important services is the authentication for a session to be established between applications. The data intended for a specific application must not be visible to another application. This process is crucial for network security because the improper implementation can lead to hackers being able to access information by impersonating an application that should have access to it.

Another important aspect is to close the session as soon as it's not required because an open session can be exploited. For this matter, fast and accurate synchronization between the applications using the session must be present.

Session Recovery

This service is so important for great user-experience using any real-time application. For example, consider a web streaming service that stopped streaming due to loss of internet connection. As soon as the internet comes back on, the web streaming should resume itself instead of requiring the user to restart the application and connect the stream.

The session layer also helps combine data originating from different application sources into one. One of the best examples of this is the video streaming where video is captured by a camera (processed and relayed through the video card), and audio is captured through the microphone (coming through the audio card), and the session layer combines them into one stream with precise synchronization before transmission to the receiver, so there's no audio/video lag at the destination.

Protocols

There are over a dozen protocols related to the session layer, each offering a specific utility. We are going to discuss two protocols briefly.

PAP

Password Authentication Protocol (PAP) is used to authenticate users using passwords. It transmits authentication information unencrypted in the network, which makes it vulnerable to attacks and not suitable for most applications. But, it is a simple protocol that is easier to learn for beginners.

SOCKS

Developed by David Koblas and available to the public in 1992, SOCKS protocol uses a proxy server to facilitate the exchange of packets over the network. For better security, the protocol supports an optional authentication feature so only intended users may have access.

The TCP/IP model, in contrast to the OSI model, doesn't have a session layer. The services are handled by HTTP.

Chapter 5: Transport Layer

The transport layer provides data transfer services to user-end applications by extending the capabilities of the network layer.

Fundamentals

Various services are provided by this layer, usually through a programming interface. We are going to look into some of the important services now.

Mux/Demux

In all modern networks, there are multiple simultaneous sockets enabled to transmit different data. This is called multiplexing and enables various applications to use the same network to transmit data. In the OSI model, this is part of the session layer, but in TCP/IP model that's used on the internet, this is present in the transport layer.

Flow Control

This is a very important service implemented in the transport layer that enables nodes with unequal speeds to communicate. This service makes sure a faster sender doesn't send data more than what the receiver can handle to avoid buffer overrun. On the other hand, it also makes sure network resources are not underutilized.

Order Correction

No network guarantees that data will be transmitted in the order it is present in the source. The transport layer actively processes packet headers and reorders packets if need be, so the destination application receives it in the intended order. The downside of this service is that the application will remain idle for a long time if the network sends the packets consistently out of order.

Congestion Control

When a packet is missed or lost, the receiver sends repeated requests to the sender to resend the packet. This is fine in normal situations, but sometimes a network can experience a high level of losses. In such situations, repeated requests can further cause congestion of available resources. Congestion control makes sure the resources are not overcommitted or over utilized, so they are available for more important tasks.

Reliability

All networks experience losses of packets and data corruption during transmission. The transport layer performs error checking using an algorithm. The transport layer also generates acknowledgment receipts upon successful and unsuccessful reception of packets.

In the OSI model, there are five protocol classes with class 0 to class 4 designation (TP0 to TP4). TP0 is ideal for error-free networks because there is no error recovery available. TP4 is closest to TCP, but the latter supports more functionalities, which are actually part of another layer in OSI.

In short, the transport layer arranges the received data, identifies and fixes errors before passing the data to the application layer. Some applications require byte transmission instead of packets over the network and application layer facilitates that as well.

Chapter 6: Network Layer

We have discussed routers and how they are used to connect several hosts in a network. The network layer encompasses that part of the network where packets are forwarded through routers.

Fundamentals

The network layer uses any and all available resources to transport the data from the source to the destination. It has no concern about any loss and errors that happen during the transfer. It acts as a bridge between the transport layer and the data link layer.

Connectionless Communication

The network layer purpose is to transmit data from one point to the other, irrespective of what happens with it or if there's an acknowledgment from the destination and what it is.

IP Addressing

Every node and end-point in a network has a fixed IP address. The network layer sends data to the intended IP address, and it's the work of upper layers (transport and session) to separate and distribute to target applications.

Router

In the real world, a network (such as the internet) is composed of smaller subnetworks connected through gateways and routers. We have discussed routers briefly before, let's see how they work in connecting different networks. These hardware devices forward packets through networks connected through them. The packets arriving at a router have the host address that it must go to. The router reads that data and forwards it to that specific address using the active routing algorithm (we are going to learn about this next). If you work in an office environment, you might have seen a device that connects all the devices in the office together. All internet connections need a router to work, which is usually installed by your ISP when you get their internet package.

A router contains two planes.

The **control plane** contains the routing algorithm and a Forward Information Base (FIB) for the other plane in the router, the **forwarding plane**. This plane forwards incoming packets to correct addresses using the information in the FIB and to match it with the information in the packet headers.

Modern routers have wireless capabilities, which means they can take data from a wired connection and forward it through a wireless connection. Below is an image of a Wifi router.

Routing Algorithms

Network layers would not be able to perform without the routing algorithms. We know that the networks are interconnected through an array of routers. The purpose of the algorithm is the find the "best" path possible to transmit the data from source to destination. To be accurate, the purpose of the network layer is to transmit the data from the router connected with the source (called first-hop router, let's call it source router for easiness) to the router connected with the destination (let's call it destination router). In most cases, the "best" path is the one that has the less cost, or which takes the least resources and time to transmit the data from source to destination router. The process gets complicated because some paths would be restricted, and even though they would have the lowest cost, the network layer wouldn't be able to use it to transmit the data.

There are different ways to categorize routing algorithms, and we will categorize algorithms in terms of how they can be updated.

Static routing algorithms update routes very slowly, and most times, only get updated through human intervention when the FIB is manually updated. **Dynamic routing algorithms** update the routes automatically depending upon the network load and/or change in path costs. Dynamic algorithms can be scheduled to run with respect to time or in response to a change in the network.

In a real-world router, especially those that are used to connect major networks, there is a combination of routing algorithms running so the router can switch the routing algorithm to adapt to different network conditions. This is another field where data science and artificial intelligence are playing a vital role in improving overall network performance.

One more thing we should learn before moving to the next chapters is the concept of virtual circuits in a network. The idea of virtual machines is very common in the digital world. When we don't have the resources of adding another real device to a system to handle additional tasks, we reserve some of the existing resources and reconfigure it as a new machine. This virtual division helps in using the same resource for multiple purposes. The same is the concept of virtual circuits where the existing circuits are reconfigured to create extra (virtual) circuits to handle more network operations.

Chapter 7: Data Link Layer

The network layer transfers data from the source router to the destination router using the best path possible. The routers themselves are connected through communication links and switches that form the data link layer. In a typical modern-day network, both wired and wireless communication links are present in the data link layer.

Fundamentals

There are various services provided by the data link layer, including the following.

Framing

Each data packet provided by the network layer is encapsulated in a frame before sending over the link. Apart from the data, the frame contains various header fields depending upon the link layer protocol used.

Link Access

In situations where multiple nodes use the same data link, a protocol named Medium Access Control (MAC) is used to specify how and which frames are transmitted over the link. In a simple network with single receiver and single sender, there is no need for MAC, and the sender can use the link whenever it is available (known as an idle link).

A link with a single sender and receiver is called a point-to-point link. A link in combining several sending and receiving nodes is called a broadcast link.

Reliable Delivery

In wireless networks where data is more prone to errors when moving through the data link, reliable delivery service ensures the errors are fixed as they happen to minimize end-to-end retransmissions to fix the errors on the receiving side. Networks that rely on wired data links, including coaxial cable and fiber optics, experience fewer errors at this layer. Therefore, a reliable delivery service is considered surplus in such networks.

Error Detection/Correction

Remember that digital bits during transmission are represented through voltage, current, or photons. And, these entities can be adversely affected by various environmental elements such as electromagnetic noise. The result can be a loss of magnitude or even reversed polarity. It is better to fix these errors at the receiving end of the data link before propagating the data packets to upper layers. How is it implemented? Error-detection bits are added to the frame, and special hardware components are added at the receiving side to use those bits to find the errors in the received frames. The special hardware components not only find the errors, but also fix them. Error detection and fixing are very sophisticated in the data link layer. But, there's a catch. What happens if the error checking bits get corrupted during frame transmission? How would the error checking hardware know if the data has errors or the error-checking bits have errors? Think about it; do some research to find out how it works.

Access and Protocols

In a network using a broadcast link, it is essential to have a protocol to make sure different nodes do not use the shared link at the same time. It is all about setting priorities. The protocols that define how the nodes in the network will share the link are called multiple access control protocols.

What happens when you are watching TV, and someone starts talking with you? You are not able to understand either of the two. The same will happen if two nodes put frames on the link at the same time. A lot of research studies have been conducted on what is the best multiple access protocol, and there are various MAC protocol categories.

Channel Partitioning protocols use communication concepts of Time Division Multiplexing (TDM) and Frequency Division Multiplexing (FDM) to divide a single link into several virtual links, each carrying different frames. This works best when several nodes need to transmit data simultaneously.

Random Access protocols make sure one node is always transmitting, and other nodes are randomly allowed to transmit. In case of a collision, the node waits a random amount of time before transmitting the frame again. Retransmission keeps happening until the frame makes it to the other end without a collision. This usually works when there is one process that requires constant, real-time network utilization, while other processes do not require immediate transmission.

Taking-turn protocols use a round-robin or daisy-chain kind of system where one node becomes the master and sends the data first. The master node then instructs other nodes one after the other to send data to the link. If the node switching is fast enough, this is actually one of the best ways to handle multiple access issues. Nodes can also be prioritized depending upon the data they have.

Switches

Up till now, we have considered that there is only one end-user (receiver) connected to a router. What if we want to connect various devices to a router? Consider your home internet service where your desktop computer, all the cell phones, tablets, laptops, and even TVs are connected to the single router provided by your ISP. How does the router transmit data to the TV, and it doesn't end up on your laptop? This is because the router provided by your ISP is not just a router, but a combination of router and switch. The switch enables various devices to be connected to the same router.

Everything connected to the switch (including the router) has a unique address called MAC address, the switch uses this address to relay information coming from the router to the intended destination. It is interesting to note that the switch remains invisible to the router and receivers. The switch also doesn't have any MAC address.

Switches can handle a finite number of device connections (each connection is created by connecting a switch adapter with the device adapter). If you have administration access to your internet router, you can actually view all the devices connected to the internal switch with their unique MAC addresses.

Switches also have the capability of sending the same data frame to all devices connected to it. This is accomplished by using a special broadcast MAC address that is recognized by all devices connected to the switch.

Data Centers

The last topic we will cover in this chapter is the data centers. To provide online services such as cloud storage, social media, and online gaming, companies built or acquired data centers. Data centers are networks made from millions of servers connected to the internet providing data storage and aggregated processing power. No doubt, data centers require a lot of setup and maintenance costs; therefore, smaller companies rent portions of data centers (called shelves/racks/slabs) from data center providers to host their services.

Each data center has multiple load balancers that distribute the load according to available hosts. In almost all cases, various services are hosted in the same data center. There are also redundant data centers that have backups and remain on standby in case the primary data center fails due to any reason.

To reduce operational costs, companies are devoting millions of dollars in research to optimize data center design. Many cost-saving techniques are already used. For example, instead of using huge HVACs to cool the data center, Google uses natural cold wind to cool down a data center thanks to its location.

Chapter 8: Physical Layer

The last of the seven-layer OSI model, the physical layer is the lowest layer from the top. This layer is related to the hardware technologies used for higher-level operations in a network.

Modulation

It is the process of changing single or multiple properties on a carrier signal, which is basically a periodic waveform, by superimposing a modulating signal that contains information that needs transmitting. Digital circuits use digital modulation, which means a discrete digital signal is used to modulate an (analog) carrier signal.

There are several digital modulation techniques, including.

1- Phase-Shift Keying (PSK) - change phase of signal

2- Frequency-Shift Keying (FSK) - change frequency of signal

3- Amplitude-Shift Keying (ASK) - change amplitude of signal

On the sending end, the signal is generated by using a modulator, which is a hardware device. Amplification and filtering is performed before data is transmitted. On the receiving end, a hardware device known as a demodulator is used to receive signal, filter, amplify, and extract bit stream, which is then passed to the data link layer.

IEEE Standards

One of the best-known IEEE standards related to the physical layer is the one that defines the physical layer of Ethernet (also known as wired Local Area Network, LAN). Ethernet has seen a lot of progress, and today it supports transmission speeds between 1 Mbps to 400 Gbps. The ethernet can be made of either coaxial cable, classic copper twisted pair, or fiber-optic wires. It is also possible the ethernet is a combination of some or all of these wires. Modern Ethernet networks are plug and play, which is supported by automatic detection of compatible settings between the connected devices. In the rare event the automatic process fails, the most common configurations are used, but that leaves the possibility of network issues.

The fastest ethernet capable of supporting speeds of up to 400 Gbps is defined in IEEE 802.3bs-2017. Note that this is maximum speed theoretically possible using the technology; in real-life, many factors can affect the performance of physical media.

Fiber optics technology uses light to transmit data. It transmits data at a very high speed, but the light amplitude drops considerably even over a short distance. It is also not possible to bend the fibers due to their delicate nature and complex transmission physics. Fiber optics require special amplifiers placed after every few amount of distance to magnify the signal. It makes the medium still a very costly medium to implement.

Equipment

There are many hardware equipment used in a network. We will discuss the two important hardware components in this chapter.

Repeater

The device used to amplify the light signal in a fiber-optic network is called a repeater. Repeaters are also used in other networks, such as cellular networks, which also experience huge signal losses. Some repeaters change the transmission method to extend signal range instead of amplifying the signal, which is more effective in certain circumstances.

Repeaters have been around since the late 1800s when they were used to extend the range of radios. Different repeaters are used for analog and digital signals. However, analog repeaters might contain digital components like electronic filters to remove various distortions in the signal.

Modem

A modem is a hardware device that performs modulation and demodulation. We have already learned what modulation and demodulation is. It is interesting to note that every computer has a modem; otherwise, it won't be able to connect to the internet.

Newer modems offer not only modulation but also operations like echo cancellation and compression. The router that your ISP provides not only contains a switch but also a modem. Actually, those routers are commonly called a modem.

With the advancement of cellular networks, companies were able to make smaller modems. Modems used in fiber optic networks are different because the modulator and demodulator still come in separate hardware packages. Modems will remain an essential part of all digital networks in the foreseeable future.

Chapter 9: Wireless and Cellular Networks

The mobility offered by wireless and cellular networks has helped them grow exponentially over the years. Now, people are not hooked to their phones at home, they are hooked to them everywhere! It has made communication faster, with many benefits for everyone. Companies have higher productivity and fewer delays because the workforce remains connected even while traveling. Parents are less anxious about the safety and security of their children, as they can communicate with them when they are not together. People can catch up with the latest news, trends, and entertainment content on the go.

It is a fact that to offer continuous mobility to its users, wireless and cellular networks deploy much more complex methods than wired networks. On top of that, these networks are more susceptible to interference from other systems, leading to more errors and losses. Let's start to learn about these networks with a few fundamental concepts.

Fundamentals

Hosts

The end user or the device at the outer edge of the network is called a (wireless) host. It might be mobile or stationary at a given time. The purpose of wireless networks is to provide supported services to all eligible hosts. What does eligibility of a host mean? It means determining whether a host gets to enjoy all (or some) network privileges depending upon its adherence to all the criteria set by the network. For example, if you don't have a high-enough account balance or if your bills are unpaid, you might not be able to make calls, but you will still be able to receive calls.

Base Station

Base stations form the frontier of wireless networks. They are the point of contact between the network and the hosts. One base station usually handles all or most of the hosts in its coverage area. A cell tower and Wireless Access Point (WAP) are base stations in cellular and wireless networks respectively. The base stations receive and relay all the information to and from the hosts. Base stations also perform a task crucial to all wireless networks that we are going to discuss next.

Handover

Every base station has a fixed coverage area. When a host starts moving towards the edge of its coverage, the network quality starts to drop. As soon as the host reaches the coverage area edge, the base station hands it over to the adjoining base station of the coverage area the host is moving into. This creates many other challenges, such as constantly determining the position of a host and distance from available base stations. Distance is not the only criteria though; a base station might be closer but working at capacity, which makes it unfit to take on another host. In reality, several base stations form overlapping coverage areas, so the hosts get handed over between different base stations without any network outage.

Every network has a certain handover capability which can fail in certain situations. For example, if the host moves faster than the handover can be made, maybe because the already overloaded neighboring base station couldn't quickly allocate resources to take on the host, in such cases network outage happens. Sometimes there are no neighboring base stations available in the direction the host is moving.

Handovers are so critical in the performance of a wireless or cellular network that most network providers actively monitor the Handover Success Rate of the network. It is a rate of successful handovers and handovers attempted. Without handovers, a wireless or cellular network is no better than a wired network.

Infrastructure

There is a complete network backbone that supports the base stations in making important decisions. For example, how does a base station know if a host should be allowed to use the network? In a cellular network, there is a special network component that keeps a log of all authorized users of the network. When a host attempts to use the network, the base station queries that special component to see if the host is allowed to use the network and to what extent. The base station allows/blocks host requests depending upon the query result. There are also many other components, including some that allow one network to communicate with another network.

The hosts, base stations, and infrastructure can be put together in different ways, giving rise to different types of wireless & cellular networks. Here are four possible network types.

Single-hop and infrastructure-based

There is a physical infrastructure consisting of a wired network to support the base stations. The base stations are directly connected to the hosts. Cellular networks are a good example.

Single-hop and infrastructure-less

There is no infrastructure; instead one of the hosts takes on the responsibilities of a base station. A Bluetooth network is a good example.

Multi-hop and infrastructure-based

The infrastructure is present to support the network, but the hosts are connected through a string of nodes after the base station to reach the infrastructure. This architecture is mostly used in sensor networks that relay information over large distances.

Multi-hop and infrastructure-less

A topic of immense research in recent years, the hosts also act as network components in the absence of a base station or infrastructure. You can say this is similar to a P2P network. This is a complex network and protocols are still being designed. This will be greatly beneficial in the Internet of Things (IoT) era.

Network Characteristics

Wireless and cellular networks differ from wired networks in many aspects. Here are a few important ones.

Deteriorating signal strength

Wireless signals have to pass through physical objects to reach hosts in wireless and cellular networks. This propagation causes drop in signal strength. In fact, wireless waves lose strength even when propagating through air. The decrease in signal strength is sometimes called path loss and increases with increasing distance between host and base station.

Interference

As already mentioned, wireless signals are more susceptible to interference. There can be different sources transmitting at the same frequency that leads to multiple signals interfering with each other. There are many electric and electronic devices (motors, microwaves, etc.) that produce electromagnetic waves. These also interfere with wireless signals.

Multipath propagation

During propagation, some or all of the wireless signals can bounce off physical objects. It means the receiver can receive echos or noise overlapping the original signal. When the host is mobile, the situation becomes even more complex and the environment constantly changes.

If you noticed, all three of the above relate to issues a wireless/cellular network can face. It is this reason protocols related to such networks heavily focus on error detection and correction. They include the CRC bit error detection codes and reliable data retransmission to compensate for missing data.

In wireless and cellular networks, we use a parameter called signal-to-noise ratio (SNR) to determine signal strength. A higher SNR makes it easier for the receiver to extract the original signal from all the background noise.

WiFi—The Wireless LAN

WiFi has become the chief source of the internet almost everywhere. Nowadays, the first thing people usually ask for when visiting someone else's place is the WiFi password. It has become a symbol of closeness! It also shows the security aspect of the wireless LAN. A password is required to connect to the WAP and use the internet service. The IEEE 802.11 group of protocols define the WiFi standard.

WiFi Standard	Supported Data Rate
802.11b	up to 11 Mbps
802.11a	up to 54 Mbps
802.11g	up to 54 Mbps (uses lower frequency range)

If you compare the supported data rates with those of wired LAN, you will notice WiFi is quite slower, but the reason it became so popular is the level of mobility it offers. It is also less expensive and faster to set up—you just need a WAP in the area where you need WiFi.

Architecture

The WiFi architecture revolves around the Base Service Set (BSS). This BSS provides an Access Point (AP, in most cases both Wireless and Wired) for other BSSs and hosts. Multiple BSSs can connect to a router to create larger/extended WiFi networks. In a typical home WiFi setup, the AP and router are combined in a single unit. There can also be signal booster devices connected to the BSS that improve signal quality in congested or narrow constructions.

In recent times, WiFi can be used to transmit data between two hosts without accessing the infrastructure or the service it provides, the internet. If you have ever connected your phone to your TV and streamed the photos in the gallery, you have already used a network referred to as "ad hoc network," a network without an AP and central control.

Identity, Association, Authentication

During installation, each AP is assigned a special Service Set Identifier (SSID). When you search for WiFi on your cell phone or laptop, you get a list of available WiFi networks, and the names you see are the SSIDs of respective WiFi network APs. You must know what the SSID of your network is so you can select and connect to the internet. Internet service providers usually put a sticker on the AP unit with the SSID and the password. The password is required so only hosts with the correct one can access the internet. In public places, such as malls, there are usually several public WiFi networks available that you can connect to and use the internet without a password.

Have you ever wondered how your cell phone or laptop finds all those WiFi networks? Every WiFi network periodically transmits beacon frames that contain the AP's SSID and MAC address. Your device scans for and receives the beacon frames and shows the information to you.

There is another way to connect the host with the AP. There is a button, usually called the WAP button, on most WiFi APs that, when pressed, sends a signal to all hosts available within range. The host can connect to the AP without the need of a password until the AP is sending the signal.

Advanced Features

Rate Adaptation

The 802.11 architecture protocols have a special rate adaptation feature that allows the network to switch the physical layer modulation technique depending upon the SNR. This is extremely useful to maintain low levels of SNR even when the host is moving inside the coverage area. A real-life example would be a child who pushes his parents for more until they have had enough. The child will wait for some time before pushing for more and the cycle continues. There are many other automated rate-adjustment designs suitable for different scenarios.

Power Management

One of the hot topics of recent times, power management is not only crucial because mobile devices have limited availability but also because less power consumption means less burden on world resources. Note that in almost every home, the WiFi APs and routers are kept on 24/7, 365 days a year which amounts to considerable power usage.

The solution is simple—automated wake and sleep capability of all nodes in a WiFi network. After being idle for a set period of time, a node will go to sleep after notifying the AP. The AP will set an alarm timer to wake up the node after a set period of time has elapsed. The AP will buffer all data packets intended for the node until the node is awake. If there are no data packets, the node will notify the AP to sleep again.

Cellular Networks

Apart from WiFi, the other major source of internet in today's world is the cellular network. Cellular networks provide even more mobility, and modern networks support very high data rates, even more than WiFi in some cases. I just signed a $50 contract with a mobile service provider that has unlimited data, call, and message services. Can you imagine unlimited data wherever you go, right in your hands? The possibilities are endless.

Generations of Cellular Networks

GSM: 2G

It all started with the modest GSM (Global System for Mobile Communications) technology, also referred to as 2G. Know why it's called cellular? Because the network is made of small coverage areas, called cells, each containing a Base Transceiver Station (BTS), which are antennas placed on the towers you might have seen along highways or on top of tall buildings. As discussed before, the coverage areas in reality are circular with overlapping regions, although in theory they are shown as hexagons and all cells perfectly together like puzzle pieces.

GSM technology revolved around voice communication, hence the modulation techniques Frequency Division Multiplexing (FDM) and Time Division Multiplexing (TDM) are used. The Base Station Controller (BSC) helps manage multiple BTSs. Both BSC and BTS are combined to form a BSS.

In revised technology versions, text and basic internet services using GPRS (Generalized Packet Radio Service) were added.

3G Networks

There are different types of 3G networks deployed in different regions of the world. The most widely available was the Universal Mobile Telecommunication Services (UMTS). Companies had invested millions of dollars in 2G networks and it wasn't feasible for them to scrap everything and adopt a completely new network technology. Designers kept that in mind when developing the 3G network. Keeping the voice communication of the 2G network the same, GPRS was upgraded, and some more nodes were added to facilitate better data transfer leading to the Wireless Edge.

Instead of just FDMA (Frequency Division Multiple Access)/TDMA (Time Division Multiple Access), 3G combines a version of CDMA, Direct Sequence Code Division Multiple Access (DS-CDMA), with TDMA slots that are present in several frequencies. In CDMA, each bit is encoded before sending using a special code (that is essentially a fast-changing signal). If you think about it, there are actually two networks working in tandem, the original 2G BSS radio network and the new 3G wireless-access network. Data rates of up to 14 Mbps were supported by this network technology.

4G LTE

The present cellular network available to most consumers, at least in the United States, is the 4G LTE (Long-Term Evolution) network. There are various distinguishing features of a 4G network, primarily the new evolved packet core (EPC) and the LTE radio access network. Talking about the EPC, it is a simplified approach that unified the two-network nature of the 3G network. The goal is to provide the best possible quality of service within the available resources. One of the best examples is the ability to depreciate the network provided to the host in order to support continuous service.

The LTE radio access network utilizes a new type of multiplexing, OFDM (Orthogonal Frequency Division Multiplexing) which is a unique integration of FDM and TDM. It enables transmission of signals using a tighter frequency spectrum without causing any interference.

Another feature that greatly enhanced network performance in 4G was the introduction of MIMO (Multiple Input, Multiple Output) antennas. The LTE network supports data rates of up to 100 Mbps (download) and 50 Mbps (upload).

Mobility Management

As mentioned earlier, mobility is the only edge cellular networks have on a wired network. The last topic of this chapter is to understand the principles that cellular networks use to determine the mobility of a host and adjust itself to maintain a constant, good-quality connection.

Let's consider the example of Amanda. She is a young, highly motivated individual who has recently graduated from college with a journalism degree. She fully believes in exploring the world and gaining different experiences first-hand. At once, she embarks on a life-transforming journey traveling from one place to another, never staying at one place for long. She is barely updating her social media, and you, as her best friend, someone who hasn't heard from her in a while, are worried. How do you contact a person whose address or phone number you don't know? Luckily, Amanda has been in constant contact with her dad because, well, someone has to pay the expenses, and you get her present address. But, since she's going to move again, you will have to contact her dad every time you want to get ahold of her (indirect). But, what if you get her number? You will be able to remain in touch most of the time (direct). Why didn't you think of that before?

The situation is quite similar when dealing with host mobility in a cellular network. The base network of a host is called the home network. When the host moves away and goes to a foreign (visited) network, the home network records the status and the present address. If another host wants to contact this host, they first are directed towards the host's home network, that redirects them to the first host's present network. In a cellular network, the identity of a host doesn't change during mobility. It is crucial, otherwise the network will not be able to track the host.

Another approach to manage mobility is to maintain a central real-time log of host locations. The mobile host will constantly beam its location to the network. This is faster because the host trying to reach the second host will not have to go to the home network and then get redirected to foreign network. It will have the other host's present location directly from the network. But, it requires considerable resources and is not feasible for large networks. The mobile host will constantly use network resources to update its location and the location log will be huge; searching and querying it will also take time and processing power.

Another approach is to support both and use the one that suits a particular situation.

Chapter 10: Networks and Multimedia

With better, cheaper internet connection comes the demand for streaming live and recorded audio and video. Today, with cable-cutting on the rise, almost every household in North America has some sort of streaming service like Netflix or Hulu. People also frequently use applications like Skype or FaceTime to do video chat where sometimes many people connect together to form a conference call—a concept that years ago was unheard of beyond corporate meeting rooms. Social media platforms such Instagram, Snapchat, and TikTok also rely heavily on video streaming.

Handling a behemoth like multimedia is a different case when it comes to networks. The amount of multimedia content created and transmitted across networks is incredible. Depending upon the requirements of the multimedia, the network can handle them differently. First we need to understand the audio and video properties involved.

Multimedia Properties

Talking about videos

Bit Rate

The most distinguishing feature of a video is its high bit rate. Even the lowest quality video conference call can require a bit rate of 100 kbps, while a typical decent-quality video stream requires 3 Mbps. The higher bit rates means a lot of data is transmitted over the network. Consider the family of Frank,

Kate, and Sasha, where everyone is using the internet together. Frank is reliving his college days by looking at memories on Facebook, Kate is streaming Desperate Housewives on Amazon Prime Video while Sasha is just FaceTiming her bff (best friend forever). Frank is looking at 1 photo every 10 seconds when each photo is roughly 350 KBs. The high definition show's stream is going on at 3 Mbps while Sasha's call is taking 500 Kbps. Considering all the activities continue to happen for an hour, here is the amount of data transferred.

Task	MBs transferred in 60 minutes
Frank's photos	126
Kate's show	10,800
Sasha's call	1800

Also, for all the activities to happen at the same time without any buffering or lagging, an internet connection of at least 4 Mbps is necessary.

Video Compression

A video is essentially images played at a fixed rate (called frame rate, where each image is taken as a frame). The most common frame rate is 24 fps (frames per second). There have been many advancements in video compression techniques over the years. The goal has been to transmit high-quality video using the lowest bit rate. One of the most widely used formats for video streaming on the internet is "mp4." More recently, many providers have shifted to the "webm" format that offers many more advantages.

Each image/frame of a video in itself is made from pixels. Every image by default has colors repeated on several areas known as spatial redundancy—for example, an image with a lot of whitespace as background. Also, different images in a sequence can have little or no difference—for example, a video shot where the PIV (Person In View) or the background doesn't move for a few seconds, which leads to temporal redundancy.

Modern video streaming services support multiple bit rates, they can automatically detect the best possible rate for your internet connection, and they stream using that rate. They also provide the option to the user to manually select a different bit rate.

Talking about audio

Audio streaming used to be the *thing* back in the days because high speed network connections that supported video streaming weren't common. Audio requires considerably less data and there are dozens of audio compression techniques that reduce file size without compromising on the audio quality. Only the most sensitive ears can pick out the difference in sound quality.

Digital audio is created by encoding analog sound waves using **sampling** and **quantization**. The quantized values are then represented by a specific number of bits. For example, if an analog sound is sampled at 16k samples per second and 8 bits are used to quantize and represent each sample, the resulting digital audio will have a bit rate of 128 Kbps. This encoding technique is very basic and known as PCM (Pulse Code Modulation).

Case Study: Netflix

There are various complex protocols and technologies to support uninterrupted video streaming over the internet. Every streaming service provider has worked on its own proprietary technology. One of the pioneers of this technology, the trend setters, the one who introduced the concept of cable-cutting and binge-watching, is Netflix. According to Sandvine, its share in US internet traffic is on the decline, thanks to the various choices now available to US consumers, but on the global level, especially in India and the Middle East, it is still on the rise.

Netflix uses different technologies for video streaming, including CDN and adaptive HTTP. The Netflix ecosystem consists of four major components:

1. Servers dedicated to registration and payment processing
2. Amazon cloud
3. Various CDN servers
4. Consumers

The only infrastructure that Netflix owns itself is made up of servers that handle user registration and authentication, capturing and charging payment methods. The Amazon cloud is used to deploy Virtual Machines (VM) to perform various functionalities.

- Processing and storing master copies of all movies and tv shows hosted by Netflix

- Processing the stored content to make it available in different video formats ideal for different consumer devices such as TVs, computers, or smartphones
- Uploading the processed versions to the CDNs located in different regions of the world

Now, let's see how this complex infrastructure is put to use by Netflix to provide the best possible UX to the consumer. When the consumer is scrolling through the Netflix directory, the information is relayed directly from the Amazon cloud. When the consumer selects and plays specific content, a manifest file is sent by Amazon cloud to the consumer client (which can be a TV, computer, or smartphone). This manifest file contains a list of all CDNs that contain the requested content in a format suitable for the client. The list is ranked, which means the best CDN is the first item on the list. The client chooses a CDN and the CDN utilizes DNS to connect the client with a specific CDN server. The client and CDN server then communicate using Dynamic Adaptive Streaming over HTTP (DASH) protocol. This manifest file is regularly updated while the consumer enjoys the content. The video data is transmitted from the CDN server to the client using approximately four-second chunks. While downloading the chunks, the client determines the quality of the next chunks to be requested in real-time using a special algorithm.

Chapter 11: Networks and Security

Network security has become a huge concern today due to a lot of private data available online. Hackers try to gain access to protected information using various tactics, with the goal to steal someone's identity or financial details. The stolen identity can later be used for blackmail and extortion.

Consequently, the need has grown exponentially for security experts who are supposed to keep data safe by designing unhackable networks. To understand what needs to be done to secure a network, we must first understand what constitutes network security.

Goals of Network Security

A secured network must guarantee the following.

Confidentiality

The transmitted information must only be accessible by the sender and receiver. Because third parties can intercept the transmission in most cases, it is important for the transmission to be encrypted, so even if someone gets ahold of the transmission, they wouldn't be able to understand the actual information.

Integrity

The transmitted information must not be changed by any malicious or accidental interference. Error-checking methods are usually used to ensure transmission integrity.

End-point authentication

The sender and receiver must be able to identify each other in a way that stops another party from assuming either one's identity. Two-factor authorization is the most recent example of end-point authentication used by online service providers.

Operational security

A network can be compromised as a whole through worms and malware that can lead to information leakage, network hijack, and DDoS attacks targeting another network. Firewalls and intrusion prevention systems are deployed by network operators to prevent all such attacks.

Introduction to Cryptography

Cryptography is as old as military forces. The first proven use of cryptography was in the era of Julias Caesar, where the Roman military gained immense advantage over enemy forces using encrypted communication. We can even consider the ancient language of Egyptian civilization (called hieroglyphs) as an encrypted language. Enemy spies could never figure out what was going on. When it comes to cryptography on the internet, the most important advancements have been in the last 30 years.

Cryptography is a vast and complex field and deserves an entirely separate book. We are going to cover only the main concepts of cryptography in this book, with relation to computer networks. The core concept is simple: before transmission, change the information (using an encryption algorithm) so an eavesdropper cannot understand the information. The receiver knows how the information was changed and uses techniques (decryption algorithm) to reconstruct the original information.

One surprising fact is that all encryption and decryption techniques used for the internet are well-documented and accessible to everyone. So, what prevents anyone from using the information to gain access to encrypted data? The reason is the use of a special encryption key that only the sender and receiver knows. The stronger the encryption key, the harder it is to decrypt the information through nefarious means. Here is a simple example of how encryption keys work. Samantha and Jason are classmates and like each other a lot. Their favorite pastime during classes? Passing notes to each other encrypted in a way that if someone catches wind of it, they wouldn't know what it actually means. What's the key? They replace all vowels in the note with the letter Z. So, when someone stumbles upon their note, it just sounds and looks like gibberish. Having said that, anyone with a bit of imagination can figure out their key and break the encryption, but imagination is not something encouraged in high schools, is it? In reality, very complex encryption techniques are used that even powerful computers cannot break without figuring out the key.

There are many different cryptographic techniques. We are going to focus on public key encryption because it solved an important security issue for computer networks and paved the way to more advanced security methods (such as digital signatures and remote authentication) used today.

Public Key Encryption

We already know that a key is the key to encryption. But, here's the dilemma: the two parties need to settle upon the encryption key before real communication can begin. It was easy for Samantha and Jason because both hang out together all day, every day. But, when it comes to computer networks, how do two remote machines settle upon a key? They will need to communicate to decide the key before using that key, potentially exposing it in the process to everyone from which the communication was supposed to be protected from!

To solve this dilemma, Diffie and Hellman built an algorithm that later became known as Diffie-Hellman Key Exchange. Let's go back to Samantha and Jason who are now network security experts. Samantha has a public key "X^+" that is visible to Jason and everyone else (including any eavesdroppers). She uses it to encrypt the message "m" and sends it to Jason. Jason receives the $X^+(m)$, just like all eavesdroppers. But, Jason has something no one else has (no lie, he really does). Jason has a private key X^- that he applies on the received message which basically means $X^-(X^+(m))$ and gets the original message. Now, it's the responsibility of Jason to guard the private key because that's the only thing stopping the eavesdroppers from figuring out the message content.

It is important to note that this encryption heavily depends on correct identification of both sender and receiver. Because Samantha's public key is available to everyone, anyone can use it to send Jason a message pretending to be her with the risk of Jason exposing his private key.

Ensuring Integrity

Making sure the message received by Jason is what Samantha sent is also absolutely crucial. The use of digital signatures is one of the most common methods used to fulfill this purpose and add authenticity to the message.

Digital Signatures

Digital signatures work the same way your signature works in real life. You sign checks and legal documents to prove that the document is yours. You might also need to sign when receiving a valuable parcel so the delivery guy has proof he handed the parcel to someone who knew your signature (that's not his fault, right?).

The concept of public and private keys can be used to digitally sign a document. We know that only Jason has the private key and if Samantha can reproduce the original message using Jason's private key, the message must have come from Jason (or Jason lost his private key).

The only difference when it comes to the use of digital signatures is the utilization of hashing. See, encrypting/decrypting messages takes a lot of computational power. The purpose of digital signatures is not to encrypt the message, so, instead of encrypting the whole message, a hash of the message is created H(m) that is always much smaller than the original message. The private key is then applied to this hashed message to create a digital signature X⁻(H(m)).

End-point Authentication

Authentication is essential to computer networks, as it allows end-users to gain access to the available services of a network. In real-life, humans use various ways to recognize another person. We recognize the face, voice, sometimes even the smell of one another. Computer networks cannot rely on human biometrics, but have their own set of digital metrics to check the authenticity of a device trying to gain access. In most cases, authentication is the first thing that happens between two networks or systems in a computer network.

There are different ways to authenticate—some simpler, some more complex—and depending upon the purpose of the network, different authentication protocols are used. Sometimes, several protocols are applied together for proper authentication. We are going to look at PGP, an authentication protocol written for emails that gained worldwide recognition, for reasons far greater than authentication and network security.

Pretty Good Privacy

As the name suggests, it was a Pretty Good Privacy (PGP) protocol for email systems. Phil Zimmermann published the scheme in 1991 as a shareware. Someone copied the protocol and published it on the internet, making it available to everyone across the world. The United States has strict censorship regulations when it comes to encryption protocols and considers export of such material as a serious crime. Phil became the target of a criminal investigation by the government that spanned three years. Eventually the case was dropped, perhaps for no better reason than it gave more exposure to Zimmermann and the US's questionable regulations. PGP is considered *the* standard when it comes to emails, although many email service providers today deploy more advanced techniques.

PGP uses a modified version of public key certification for authentication. Users of PGP can trust public keys as authentic and can allow other users to authenticate keys on their behalf. There are key-signing parties where people meet and exchange public keys by signing them with their private keys.

The PGP service provides services of both digital signatures and encryption. It uses either MD5 or SHA, depending upon the platform the software is being used on, IDEA, triple-DES, or CAST for key encryption, and RSA to encrypt public keys.

Chapter 12: Networks and Management

Computer networks are made up of complex systems interacting with each other using special protocols. There are hardware and software sides of a network. It is a given fact that in such a huge system, something can malfunction anytime. The job of network management (usually a team of network administrators) is to make sure such issues are fixed as soon as possible and to guarantee future occurrences will not happen. Network administrators use a wide range of tools to monitor, diagnose, and fix network issues. This chapter is dedicated to explaining all such protocols in a concise and simple way.

Network Topology

Network topology defines how different nodes are joined together to create a network. It is essentially a schematic description. Different topologies have different pros and cons, so the intended use of the network will dictate which topology to use.

Bus Topology

Each node in the network is connected through a single cable. The data can travel only in one direction at a time through a network using bus topology.

Advantages

1. Cheap
2. Easy to troubleshoot

3. Easy to expand

Disadvantages

1. Cable fault means whole network failure
2. Not suitable for heavy network traffic
3. Slower

Ring Topology

A ring is formed by connecting each node to the next one and the last one is connected to the first node. Each node has two neighbors. Only nodes with a token can transmit data. This is also the most common type of daisy-chain topology.

Advantages

1. Inexpensive installation and expansion
2. Supports heavy traffic

Disadvantages

1. One node failure affects the entire network
2. Troubleshooting is difficult

Star Topology

A single hub is used as the central point of contact for all the nodes. Nodes are not connected directly to each other.

Advantages

1. Faster data transmission
2. More control on traffic flow
3. One node failure doesn't affect the entire network

Disadvantages

1. High hardware cost
2. Failure of the hub breaks the entire network
3. Network performance limited by hub capacity

Mesh Topology

All nodes are interconnected with a lot of redundancy, meaning less network failure. If nodes are directly connected to one another, it's called flooding. If nodes are routed using a predefined logic, it's called "routing."

Advantages

1. Robust
2. Better load distribution

Disadvantages

1. Difficult to deploy and configure
2. Hardware cost is considerable

Tree Topology

One node acts as the root and all other nodes branch out, increasing as the levels go deeper. Also known as hierarchical topology, there must be at least three levels.

Advantages

1. Best for joining grouped nodes
2. Ideal for very large networks
3. Easily extendable

Disadvantages

1. Hardware cost is high
2. Maintenance can be challenging
3. Root of the tree is critical for network stability

There is also a hybrid topology where different topologies are mixed together to create a network.

Responsibilities of Network Management

The list of network management needs is ever-expanding, yet with great progress in data analysis and artificial intelligence, many of the following have been automated without the need of a human touch.

Pinpoint Source of Issue

It is essential to find where any issue is coming from. This is usually taken care by automated tools that the network components use to generate tickets signifying that a specific component has failed.

Active Monitoring

Instead of relying on the consumer to report an issue, network management actively scans the network for potential downgradations and proactively fixes them.

Resource Deployment

There is usually a different department that plans and deploys resources in the network. The job of network management is to identify and project specific demands in a network and relay the information to the concerned department. In modern wireless networks, service providers share the same infrastructure to lower operational costs. Network management might have to interact with another provider if the equipment that has malfunctioned belongs to them.

KPI Monitoring

Every network operator has to ensure the KPIs (Key Performance Indicators) are maintained in the range agreed in the SLA (Service Level Agreement). For example, the telecom company I interned at had several KPIs to maintain; one was the Handover Success Rate (HSR), which must be above 99% through the entire network.

Network Management Infrastructure

The last thing we are going to discuss in this chapter is the infrastructure needed for proper network management. Network management forms the umbrella that covers all the aspects and parts of the network architecture. Network management usually uses a different terminology to identify network components than what they are known by to other network components.

A Management Information Base (MIB) is used to collect all the information about the network that is usually condensed to show overall trends. It helps in making decisions that will affect the entire network—for example, if a certain network area is experiencing overload and requires more nodes.

Another important piece of network management infrastructure is the network management protocol. It enables the management to query specific parts of the network to gather information. It helps the network management to determine if a specific team (such as maintenance or optimization) needs to prioritize an issue.

Modern network technologies have made the entire management process almost automatic and controlled through software. Instead of dozens of administrators working on managing the network, only a couple of them are now enough to oversee an entire region's network. Network data is continuously collected, trends determined, and actionable information is relayed to network components that adjust themselves accordingly. Reports are also generated for future reference and sent to the human team for analysis.

Conclusion

Computer networks are an ever-evolving field. The next best thing is the Internet of Things (IoT) that is potentially changing how people live their lives. The concept is simple: everything in this world will be connected to the internet. It is only possible when all technologies will be compatible with each other. It is a difficult idea because many systems have different standards. But, what if we achieve a global standardization that guarantees maximum compatibility, IoT will bring a huge change in everyone's lives.

You might have already seen a SciFi movie or TV show where the concept of 'smart homes,' 'smart cars' and 'sentient robots' have been shown. Most would assume that the most achievable of these concepts in our lifetime would be the smart home because a lot of these devices are already available on today's market. With this developed technology one will be able to control and automate every aspect of a home using your voice, hand gestures, or linked smart devices.

There are, of course, serious concerns in the domain of privacy and security because those areas are still not developed to the required level. But, with time, these issues will be solved to the degree that the majority of the global population will be confident in adopting the technology. It is important to note that even with the latest security features used by companies on the internet, nothing is 100% safe. People still use the internet, and in fact, the usage is growing even faster than before.

The idea of smart devices started when a Coke vending machine in a university became the first application connected with the internet in 1982. There have been many research and study papers on the topic. There is no doubt the applications are numerous, including better healthcare and improved transportation.

Different technical standards are currently being referenced for the development of IoT design. The standards themselves are a work in progress. One of the reasons IoT has become a mainstream concept is the progress made in the field of data science. IoT is heavily dependent on data collection, processing, and results obtained from it. This dependency has given rise to the issue of privacy and security. What is the boundary of privacy? How much is a person willing to share with a system that might get compromised? Who will be responsible for such an incident? In today's world, companies have to pay millions of dollars in damages in case of a data breach.

Recently, Facebook, Google, and Amazon have announced a partnership to create a standard framework, so it will be easier to connect their technologies. This is a big step towards a real implementation of IoT. How well that will work out and which company will develop which part of the network is still to be seen but here's another dilemma, people already distrust these large global business entities. Would they trust them with more private data considering there's no current law that encompasses these new technologies? We have seen that Europe has always been at the forefront of creating new standards and regulations to handle the adoption of new technologies better. We are still to see any European Union body to release a major decision regarding IoT.

All of this would mean nothing without proper regulations implemented by governments all over the world. All technologies take time to propagate, but this one technology would mean little if everything is not connected to the internet.

The lack of trust between governments has already seen technologies being regarded as dangerous. On top of that, IoT will generate huge amounts of data that will need to be processed and stored if necessary. Major improvements are needed in storage technologies to handle the expected requirements. Another problem is the impact on the environment and health of the users. There are already concerns about the increased use of electronics and signals all around us, having a gradual bad effect on the health and environment.

There is no doubt it will take decades for the public to see IoT in its full glory. What will happen in those decades will decide how revolutionary it will be. In my opinion, a bigger breakthrough would be the discovery of a better material to replace the obsolete and saturated silicon as the base of all electronic devices.

References

Clement, J. (2019). Global Digital Population 2019. Retrieved from https://www.statista.com/statistics/617136/digital-population-worldwide/

Lowe, D. (2008). Networking all-in-one desk reference for dummies: For Dummies S (1st ed.). Indianapolis, IN.

Naste, R. (2018). Computer Networking for Beginners: Your Guide for Mastering Computer Networking, Cisco Ios and the Osi Model (Computer Networking Series).

Tanenbaum, A. S., & Wetherall, D. J. (1988). Computer networks (5th ed.). Englewood Cliffs, NJ: Prentice Hall.

Printed in Great Britain
by Amazon

17968299R00068